M000106003

Guided Reading and
Review Workbook

Prentice
Hall

Needham, Massachusetts
Upper Saddle River, New Jersey
Glenview, Illinois

ISBN 0-13-067947-X

2 3 4 5 6 7 8 9 10   06 05 04 03 02

TABLE OF CONTENTS

Unit 4: Money, Banking, and Finance

Unit 5: Measuring Economic Performance

Unit 6: Government and the Economy

Unit 7: The Global Economy

Success in social studies comes from doing three things well—reading, testing, and writing. The following pages present strategies to help you read for meaning, understand test questions, and write well.

Reading for Meaning

Do you have trouble remembering what you read? Here are some tips from experts that will improve your ability to recall and understand what you read:

BEFORE YOU READ

Preview the text to identify important information.
Like watching the coming attractions at a movie theater, previewing the text helps you know what to expect. Study the questions and strategies below to learn how to preview what you read.

Ask yourself these questions:	Use these strategies to find the answers:
• What is the text about?	Read the headings, subheadings, and captions. Study the photos, maps, tables, or graphs.
• What do I already know about the topic?	Read the questions at the end of the text to see if you can answer any of them.
• What is the purpose of the text?	Turn the headings into *who, what, when, where, why,* or *how* questions. This will help you decide if the text compares things, tells a chain of events, or explains causes and effects.

AS YOU READ

Organize information in a way that helps you see meaningful connections or relationships.

Taking notes as you read will improve your understanding. Use graphic organizers like the ones below to record the information you read. Study these descriptions and examples to learn how to create each type of organizer.

Sequencing

A **flowchart** helps you see how one event led to another. It can also display the steps in a process.

Use a flowchart if the text—
• tells about a chain of events.
• explains a method of doing something.

TIP▶ List the events or steps in order.

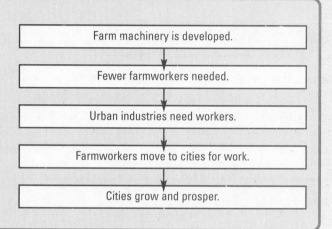

Comparing and Contrasting

A **Venn diagram** displays similarities and differences.

Use a Venn diagram if the text—
• compares and contrasts two individuals, groups, places, things, or events.

TIP▶ Label the outside section of each circle and list differences.
Label the shared section and list similarities.

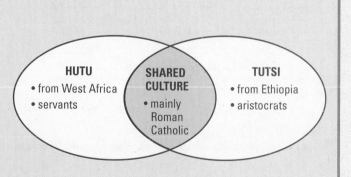

Categorizing Information

A **chart** organizes information in categories.

Use a chart if the text—
- lists similar facts about several places or things.
- presents characteristics of different groups.

TIP▶ Write an appropriate heading for each column in the chart to identify its category.

COUNTRY	FORM OF GOVERNMENT	ECONOMY
Cuba	communist dictatorship	command economy
Puerto Rico	democracy	free enterprise system

Identifying Main Ideas and Details

A **concept web** helps you understand relationships among ideas.

Use a concept web if the text—
- provides examples to support a main idea.
- links several ideas to a main topic.

TIP▶ Write the main idea in the largest circle. Write details in smaller circles and draw lines to show relationships.

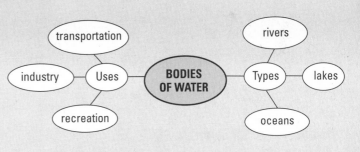

Organizing Information

An **outline** provides an overview, or a kind of blueprint for reading.

Use an outline to organize ideas—
- according to their importance.
- according to the order in which they are presented.

TIP▶ Use Roman numerals for main ideas, capital letters for secondary ideas, and Arabic numerals for supporting details.

> **I. Differences Between the North and the South**
>   **A.** Views on slavery
>   **1.** Northern abolitionists
>   **2.** Southern slave owners
>   **B.** Economies
>   **1.** Northern manufacturing
>   **2.** Southern agriculture

Identifying Cause and Effect

A **cause-and-effect** diagram shows the relationship between what happened (effect) and the reason why it happened (cause).

Use a cause-and-effect chart if the text—
- lists one or more causes for an event.
- lists one or more results of an event.

TIP▶ Label causes and effects. Draw arrows to indicate how ideas are related.

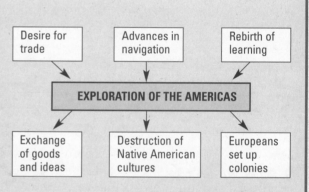

AFTER YOU READ

Test yourself to find out what you learned from reading the text.

Go back to the questions you asked yourself before you read the text. You should be able to give more complete answers to these questions:
- What is the text about?
- What is the purpose of the text?

You should also be able to make connections between the new information you learned from the text and what you already knew about the topic.

Study your graphic organizer. Use this information as the *answers*. Make up a meaningful *question* about each piece of information.

Taking Tests

Do you panic at the thought of taking a standardized test? Here are some tips that most test developers recommend to help you achieve good scores.

MULTIPLE-CHOICE QUESTIONS

Read each part of a multiple-choice question to make sure you understand what is being asked.

Many tests are made up of multiple-choice questions. Some multiple-choice items are **direct questions.** They are complete sentences followed by possible answers, called distractors.

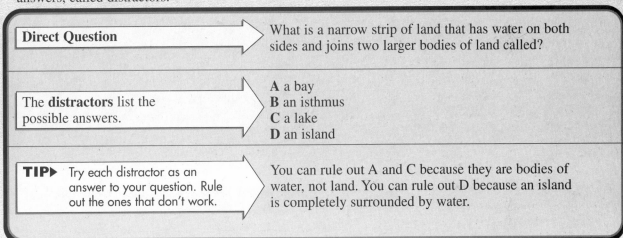

Direct Question	What is a narrow strip of land that has water on both sides and joins two larger bodies of land called?
The **distractors** list the possible answers.	A a bay B an isthmus C a lake D an island
TIP▶ Try each distractor as an answer to your question. Rule out the ones that don't work.	You can rule out A and C because they are bodies of water, not land. You can rule out D because an island is completely surrounded by water.

Other multiple-choice questions are **incomplete sentences** that you are to finish. They are followed by possible answers.

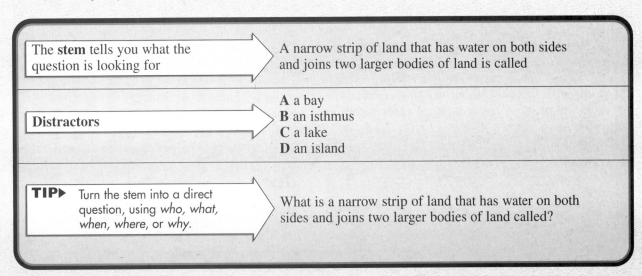

The **stem** tells you what the question is looking for	A narrow strip of land that has water on both sides and joins two larger bodies of land is called
Distractors	A a bay B an isthmus C a lake D an island
TIP▶ Turn the stem into a direct question, using *who, what, when, where,* or *why.*	What is a narrow strip of land that has water on both sides and joins two larger bodies of land called?

WHAT'S BEING TESTED?

Identify the type of question you are being asked.

Social studies tests often ask questions that involve reading comprehension. Other questions may require you to gather or interpret information from a map, graph, or chart. The following strategies will help you answer different kinds of questions.

Reading Comprehension Questions

What to do:

How to do it:

1. Determine the content and organization of the selection.

Read the **title.** Skim the selection. Look for key words that indicate time, cause-and-effect, or comparison.

2. Analyze the questions.
   Do they ask you to *recall facts?*

Look for **key words** in the stem:
According to the selection . . .
The selection states that . . .

   Do they ask you to *make judgments?*

The main idea of the selection is . . .
The author would likely agree that . . .

3. Read the selection.

Read quickly. Keep the questions in mind.

4. Answer the questions.

Try out each distractor and choose the best answer. Refer back to the selection if necessary.

Example:

A Region of Diversity The Khmer empire was one of many kingdoms in Southeast Asia. Unlike the Khmer empire, however, the other kingdoms were small because Southeast Asia's mountains kept people protected and apart. People had little contact with those who lived outside their own valley.

Why were most kingdoms in Southeast Asia small?
A disease killed many people
B lack of food
C climate was too hot
D mountains kept people apart

TIP▶ The key word <u>because</u> tells why the kingdoms were small.
(The correct answer is D.)

Map Questions

What to do:	How to do it:
1. Determine what kind of information is presented on the map.	Read the map **title.** It will indicate the purpose of the map. Study the **map key.** It will explain the symbols used on the map. Look at the **scale.** It will help you calculate distance between places on the map.
2. Read the question. Determine which component on the map will help you find the answer.	Look for **key words** in the stem. About <u>how far</u> . . . [use the scale] <u>What crops</u> were grown in . . . [use the map key]
3. Look at the map and answer the question in your own words.	Do not read the distractors yet.
4. Choose the best answer.	Decide which distractor agrees with the answer you determined from the map.

Eastern Europe: Language Groups

In which of these countries are Thraco-Illyrian languages spoken?

A Romania
B Albania
C Hungary
D Lithuania

TIP▶ Read the labels and the key to understand the map.
(The correct answer is B.)

KEY

- Slavic languages
- Romance languages
- Thraco-Illyrian languages
- Baltic languages
- Non-Indo-European languages

Lambert Azimuthal Equal-Area Projection

Graph Questions

What to do:

1. Determine the purpose of the graph.

2. Determine what information on the graph will help you find the answer.

3. Choose the best answer.

How to do it:

Read the graph **title.** It indicates what the graph represents.

Read the **labels** on the graph or on the key. They tell the units of measurement used by the graph.

Decide which distractor agrees with the answer you determined from the graph.

Example

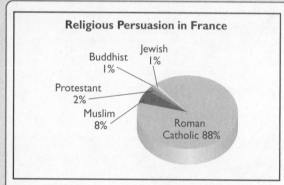

A **Circle graph** shows the relationship of parts to the whole in terms of percentages.

After Roman Catholics, the next largest religious population in France is

A Buddhist   C Jewish
B Protestant   D Muslim

TIP▶ Compare the percentages listed in the labels. (The correct answer is D.)

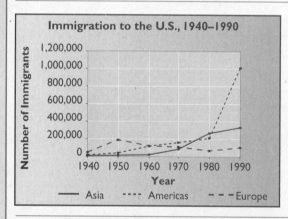

A **line graph** shows a pattern or change over time by the direction of the line.

Between 1980 and 1990, immigration to the U.S. from the Americas

A decreased a little   C stayed about the same
B increased greatly   D increased a little

TIP▶ Compare the vertical distance between the two correct points on the line graph.
(The correct answer is B.)

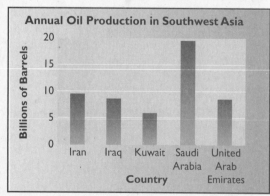

A **bar graph** compares differences in quantity by showing bars of different lengths.

Saudi Arabia produces about how many more billion of barrels of oil a year than Iran?

A 5 million   C 15 million
B 10 million   D 20 million

TIP▶ Compare the heights of the bars to find the difference.
(The correct answer is B.)

Writing for Social Studies

When you face a writing assignment, do you think, "How will I ever get through this?" Here are some tips to guide you through any writing project from start to finish.

THE WRITING PROCESS

Follow each step of the writing process to communicate effectively.

Step 1. Prewrite

- Establish the purpose.
- Define the topic.
- Determine the audience.
- Gather details.

Step 2. Draft

- Organize information logically in an outline or graphic organizer.
- Write an introduction, body, and conclusion.
- State main ideas clearly.
- Include relevant details to support your ideas.

Step 3. Revise

- Edit for clarity of ideas and elaboration.

Step 4. Proofread

- Correct any errors in spelling, grammar, and punctuation.

Step 5. Publish and Present

- Copy text neatly by hand, or use a typewriter or word processor.
- Illustrate as needed.
- Create a cover, if appropriate.

TYPES OF WRITING FOR SOCIAL STUDIES

Identify the purpose for your writing.

Each type of writing assignment has a specific purpose, and each purpose needs a different plan for development. The following descriptions and examples will help you identify the three purposes for social studies writing. The lists of steps will help you plan your writing.

Writing to Inform

Purpose: to present facts or ideas

Example

During the 1960s, research indicated the dangers of the insecticide DDT. It killed insects but also had long-term effects. When birds and fish ate poisoned insects, DDT built up in their fatty tissue. The poison also showed up in human beings who ate birds and fish contaminated by DDT.

TIP▶ Look for these **key terms** in the assignment: explain, describe, report, narrate

How to get started:
- Determine the topic you will write about.
- Write a topic sentence that tells the main idea.
- List all the ideas you can think of that are related to the topic.
- Arrange the ideas in logical order.

Writing to Persuade

Purpose: to influence someone

Example

Teaching computer skills in the classroom uses time that could be spent teaching students how to think for themselves or how to interact with others. Students who can reason well, express themselves clearly, and get along with other people will be better prepared for life than those who can use a computer.

TIP▶ Look for these **key terms** in the assignment: convince, argue, request

How to get started:
- Make sure you understand the problem or issue clearly.
- Determine your position.
- List evidence to support your arguments.
- Predict opposing views.
- List evidence you can use to overcome the opposing arguments.

Writing to Provide Historical Interpretations

Purpose: to present the perspective of someone in a different era

Example

The crossing took a week, but the steamship voyage was hard. We were cramped in steerage with hundreds of others. At last we saw the huge statue of the lady with the torch. In the reception center, my mother held my hand while the doctor examined me. Then, my father showed our papers to the official, and we collected our bags. I was scared as we headed off to find a home in our new country.

TIP▶ Look for these **key terms** in the assignment: go back in time, create, suppose that, if you were

How to get started:
- Study the events or issues of the time period you will write about.
- Consider how these events or issues might have affected different people at the time.
- Choose a person whose views you would like to present.
- Identify the thoughts and feelings this person might have experienced.

RESEARCH FOR WRITING

Follow each step of the writing process to communicate effectively.

After you have identified the purpose for your writing, you may need to do research. The following steps will help you plan, gather, organize, and present information.

Step 1. Ask Questions

Ask yourself questions to help guide your research.	What do I already know about the topic? What do I want to find out about the topic?

Step 2. Acquire Information

Locate and use appropriate sources of information about the topic.	Library Internet search Interviews
Take notes.	Follow accepted format for listing sources.

Step 3. Analyze Information

Evaluate the information you find.	Is it relevant to the topic? Is it up-to-date? Is it accurate? Is the writer an authority on the topic? Is there any bias?

Step 4. Use Information

Answer your research questions with the information you have found. (You may find that you need to do more research.)	Do I have all the information I need?
Organize your information into the main points you want to make. Identify supporting details.	Arrange ideas in outline form or in a graphic organizer.

Step 5. Communicate What You've Learned

Review the purpose for your writing and choose an appropriate way to present the information.	Purpose	Presentation
	inform	formal paper, documentary, multimedia
	persuade	essay, letter to the editor, speech
	interpret	journal, newspaper account, drama
Draft and revise your writing, and then evaluate it.	Use a rubric for self-evaluation.	

EVALUATING YOUR WRITING

Use the following rubric to help you evaluate your writing.

	Excellent	Good	Acceptable	Unacceptable
Purpose	Achieves purpose—to inform, persuade, or provide historical interpretation—very well	Informs, persuades, or provides historical interpretation reasonably well	Reader cannot easily tell if the purpose is to inform, persuade, or provide historical interpretation	Lacks purpose
Organization	Develops ideas in a very clear and logical way	Presents ideas in a reasonably well-organized way	Reader has difficulty following the organization	Lacks organization
Elaboration	Explains all ideas with facts and details	Explains most ideas with facts and details	Includes some supporting facts and details	Lacks supporting details
Use of Language	Uses excellent vocabulary and sentence structure with no errors in spelling, grammar, or punctuation	Uses good vocabulary and sentence structure with very few errors in spelling, grammar, or punctuation	Includes some errors in grammar, punctuation, and spelling	Includes many errors in grammar, punctuation, and spelling

Section 1: Guided Reading and Review
Scarcity and the Factors of Production

A. As You Read
As you read Section 1, supply in the space provided an explanation an economist might give showing why each statement is true.

Statement	Explanation

Statement

1. People must make choices to satisfy their needs and wants.

2. Scarcity always exists.

3. Physical capital is an important factor of production.

4. All goods and services are scarce.

5. Entrepreneurs are important to the production of goods and services.

Explanation

1. _____

_____

2. _____

_____

3. _____

_____

4. _____

_____

5. _____

_____

B. Reviewing Key Terms
Complete each sentence by writing the correct term in the blank.

6. A CD player is a _____ rather than a need because it is not necessary to survival.

7. The study of how people seek to meet their needs and wants by making choices is _____.

8. Persons who perform such actions as cutting hair or teaching school are providing _____.

9. When producers will not or cannot offer goods and services at current prices, a _____ occurs.

10. Land, labor, and capital make up the _____.

11. When people make resources for producing other goods and services they are creating _____.

12. The term _____ refers to water, forests, and all other natural resources used to produce goods and services.

13. The two categories of capital are physical and _____.

14. Factories, machinery, and pencils are all examples of _____ capital.

15. Leaders who take risks to develop original ideas and start new industries are called _____.

Section 2: Guided Reading and Review
Opportunity Cost

A. As You Read

As you read Section 2, fill in two supporting facts or details under each main idea by answering each question.

Main Idea: Trade-offs are alternatives that people give up when they choose one course of action over another.

1. Who makes trade-offs? _____

2. Why do decisions involve trade-offs? _____

Main Idea: Opportunity cost is the most desirable alternative given up as the result of a decision.

3. How does opportunity cost vary? _____

4. Why does opportunity cost vary? _____

Main Idea: Deciding whether to do or use one more or one less unit of some resource is thinking at the margin.

5. What does thinking at the margin help with? _____

6. What does thinking at the margin help compare? _____

_____

B. Reviewing Key Terms

Answer each of the following questions.

7. In what way are trade-offs and opportunity costs alike?

_____

_____

8. How does an opportunity cost differ from a trade-off?

_____

_____

9. What are "guns or butter" decisions?

_____

_____

10. How does thinking at the margin change the decision-making process?

_____

_____

_____

Section 3: Guided Reading and Review
Production Possibilities Curves

A. As You Read
As you read Section 3, complete the chart by indicating where on a production possibilities curve the following information is shown.

Reading a Production Possibilities Curve

1. Categories or specific goods or services to be compared

_____

2. Range of choices in the combination of goods or services produced

_____

3. Production possibilities frontier

_____

4. An economy working at its most efficient production levels

_____

5. An economy working below its most efficient production levels

_____

6. Future production possibilities frontier if more land, labor, or capital resources become available

_____

B. Reviewing Key Terms
Define the following terms.

7. production possibilities curve _____

8. production possibilities frontier _____

9. efficiency _____

10. underutilization _____

11. cost _____

12. law of increasing costs _____

Section 1: Guided Reading and Review
Answering the Three Economic Questions

A. As You Read

As you read Section 1, supply the missing information about economic systems in the spaces provided.

1. Three economic questions answered:

    (a) _____

    (b) _____

    (c) _____

2. Economic concept necessitating choices and priorities in any society:

    _____

3. Economic question answered by basic social values and goals:

    _____

4. Five basic economic goals guiding society's choice of systems:

    (a) _____

    (b) _____

    (c) _____

    (d) _____

    (e) _____

5. Four main kinds of economies:

    (a) _____   (c) _____

    (b) _____   (d) _____

B. Reviewing Key Terms

Complete each sentence by writing the correct term in the blank.

6. An economic system that relies on habit, custom, or ritual to decide questions of production and consumption of goods and services is a _____.

7. An encyclopedia entry illustrating how a hunter-gatherer group collects and shares food resources is describing that society's _____.

8. When voluntary exchanges in the markets determine decisions on production and consumption, the society's economic system is a _____.

9. When people earn income for supplying land, labor, capital, or entrepreneurship, they receive _____.

10. An economic system in which the central government makes all decisions on production and consumption of goods and services is a _____.

11. People who receive disaster relief from the government after a flood are benefiting from an economic system that provides a _____.

Section 2: Guided Reading and Review
The Free Market

A. As You Read
As you read Section 2, list the role or roles played in a free market economy by each factor in the diagram below.

Roles and Functions in a Free Market Economy

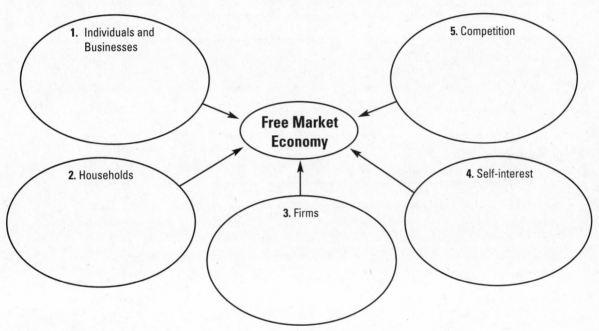

1. Individuals and Businesses

5. Competition

Free Market Economy

2. Households

3. Firms

4. Self-interest

B. Reviewing Key Terms
Match the definitions in Column I with the terms in Column II. Write the letter of the correct answer in the blank provided. You will not use all of the terms.

Column I

_____ **6.** market in which households purchase the goods and services that firms produce

_____ **7.** an expectation that encourages people to behave in a certain way

_____ **8.** power of consumers to decide what gets produced

_____ **9.** market in which firms purchase the factors of production from households

_____ **10.** financial gain made in a transaction

_____ **11.** concentration of productive efforts of individuals and firms on a limited number of activities

_____ **12.** an arrangement that allows for exchange among buyers and sellers

Column II

a. profit

b. competition

c. product market

d. market

e. incentive

f. self-interest

g. specialization

h. factor market

i. consumer sovereignty

Section 3: Guided Reading and Review
Centrally Planned Economies

A. As You Read
As you read Section 3, supply the missing information in the chart below.

Central Economic Planning in the Former Soviet Union

1. Main goal: _____
   _____
   _____

2. Role of central government:
   (a) _____
   (b) _____
   _____

3. Effects on agriculture:
   (a) *Positive* _____
   (b) *Negative* _____

4. Effects on industry:
   (a) *Positive* _____
   (b) *Negative* _____

5. Effects on consumers:
   (a) *Positive* _____
   (b) *Negative* _____

B. Reviewing Key Terms
Define the following terms.

6. socialism _____
   _____

7. communism _____
   _____

8. authoritarian _____
   _____

9. collective _____
   _____

10. heavy industry _____
    _____

Section 4: Guided Reading and Review
Modern Economies

A. As You Read

As you read Section 4, fill in two supporting facts or details under each main idea by answering each question.

Main Idea: Government intervenes in market economies because some needs and wants of modern societies are hard to answer in the marketplace or may be answered more fairly for all members of society with government involvement.

1. What needs and wants are hard to answer? _____

   _____

2. What needs and wants are answered more fairly with government involvement?

   _____

   _____

Main Idea: Government intervention dominates in some mixed economies.

3. How does government intervene in North Korea's economy? _____

   _____

4. How is government intervention less extreme in China's economy? _____

   _____

Main Idea: The market system dominates in some mixed economies.

5. Where is the world's freest market located? _____

   _____

6. Why is it one of the freest? _____

   _____

B. Reviewing Key Terms

Answer each of the following questions.

7. How does *free enterprise* differ from *laissez faire*? _____

   _____

8. Why is China said to have a *transition* economy? _____

   _____

9. What does it mean to *privatize* an industry? _____

   _____

10. Why do the world's national economies fall inside a *continuum*? _____

   _____

Section 1: Guided Reading and Review
Benefits of Free Enterprise

A. As You Read

As you read Section 1, supply the missing information about the American market system in the spaces provided.

Free Enterprise

Basic principles:

1. _____
2. _____
3. _____
4. _____
5. _____
6. _____
7. _____

Consumer

Basic Roles:

8. _____
9. _____

Government

Basic Roles:

10. _____
11. _____
12. _____
13. _____

B. Reviewing Key Terms

Complete each sentence by writing the correct key term in the blank.

14. When individuals decide to put their house up for sale, they are exercising their _____.

15. Farmers who feel they need a private organization to influence public policy in their behalf might form a/an _____.

16. Nutritional values printed on candy wrappers or milk cartons are required under _____.

17. The concerns of the public as a whole make up the _____.

NAME _____ CLASS _____ DATE _____

A. As You Read
As you read Section 2, supply the requested information in the spaces provided.

1. Usual length of the business cycle: _____

_____

_____

2. Three main outcomes of public policy aimed at economic stability: _____

_____

_____

3. Requirement for raising living standards for new generations: _____

_____

_____

4. Two indicators of economic stability: _____

_____

_____

5. Government-provided incentives for innovation: _____

_____

_____

B. Reviewing Key Terms
Define the following terms.

6. macroeconomics _____

_____

7. microeconomics _____

_____

_____

8. business cycle _____

_____

_____

9. gross domestic product _____

_____

_____

10. technology _____

_____

_____

Section 3: Guided Reading and Review
Providing Public Goods

A. As You Read

As you read Section 3, fill in two supporting facts or details under each main idea by answering each question.

Main Idea: In some situations, the free market does not efficiently distribute resources.

1. What is an example of something that self-interest would not motivate consumers to provide?

_____

2. Why might this public good be unreasonable to expect from private providers?

_____

Main Idea: Cost is an important factor in determining whether a good or service is produced as a public good.

3. How does this factor relate to the individual? _____

_____

4. How does this factor relate to society? _____

_____

Main Idea: A good or service can generate positive or negative side effects for people who do not pay for or produce them.

5. What is an example of a positive side effect? _____

6. What is an example of a negative side effect? _____

B. Reviewing Key Terms

Match the definitions in Column I with the terms in Column II. Write the letter of the correct answer in the blank provided.

Column I

_____ 7. shared good or service for which it would be impractical to make consumers pay individually and to exclude nonpayers

_____ 8. situation in which the free market does not distribute resources efficiently

_____ 9. part of the economy that involves the transactions of the government

_____ 10. part of the economy involving transactions of individuals and businesses

_____ 11. economic side effect of a good or service that generates unintended benefits or costs to someone other than the person deciding how much to produce or consume

_____ 12. someone who would not choose to pay for a certain good or service, but who can still reap the benefits of it anyway if it is a public good

Column II

a. externality

b. public sector

c. market failure

d. public good

e. free rider

f. private sector

NAME _____ CLASS _____ DATE _____

A. As You Read
As you read Section 4, supply the missing information in the chart below.

Tax-Supported Safety Nets		
Program or Program Area	**Form of Aid**	**Recipients**
1. TANF		
2. Social Security		
3.		Workers who are laid off or lose their jobs
4. Worker's Compensation		
5.	Health insurance	
6. Education		

B. Reviewing Key Terms
Rewrite each statement below to make it agree with the italicized key term.

7. The most common *in-kind benefits* include food giveaways, food stamps, subsidized housing, and farm aid. _____

_____

_____

8. The government institutes *welfare* programs to improve transportation routes. _____

_____

_____

9. A nation's *standard of living* indicates its level of income distribution. _____

_____

_____

10. The *poverty threshold* is the income level below that which is needed to provide the needs and wants of families or households. _____

_____

_____

_____

Section 1: Guided Reading and Review
Understanding Demand

A. As You Read

As you read Section 1, for each boxed example, fill in the key term the example illustrates in the space provided.

1. the higher the price of pizza, the fewer slices people will buy	2. eating salad or tacos instead of pizza when the price of pizza goes up	3. buying fewer slices of pizza when rising prices reduce real income
_____	_____	_____

4.	Price	Quantity
	1	5
	2	4
	3	3
	4	2
	_____	

5.	Price	Quantity
	1	300
	2	250
	3	200
	4	150
	_____	

B. Reviewing Key Terms

Complete each sentence by writing the correct term in the blank.

6. A _____ is a table that lists the quantities of a good a person will buy at each price that may be offered in the market.

7. A _____ is a table that lists the quantities of a good demanded by all consumers at each price that may be offered in the market.

8. A _____ is a graphical representation of a demand schedule.

9. The _____ is the change in consumption resulting from a change in real income.

10. The _____ says that when a good's price is lower, consumers will buy more of it.

NAME _____ CLASS _____ DATE _____

A. As You Read

As you read Section 2, answer the following questions in the space provided.

1. What condition must exist to make a demand curve accurate? _____

_____

_____

2. What happens to a demand curve when there is a change in factors (other than price) that
can affect consumers' decisions about purchasing the good? _____

_____

3. How does consumer income affect the demand for normal and inferior goods? _____

_____

4. How does consumer expectation affect demand for certain goods? _____

_____

_____

5. Explain how the baby boom generation affected demand for certain goods. _____

_____

_____

6. How are consumer tastes and advertising related? _____

_____

_____

7. Explain how demand for a good can affect demand for a related good. _____

_____

_____

8. Give an example of a substitute good. _____

B. Reviewing Key Terms

Match the definitions in Column I with the terms in Column II. Write the letter of the correct
answer in the blank provided.

Column I	Column II
_____ 9. all other things held constant	a. normal goods
_____ 10. goods whose demand increases as consumer income increases	b. substitutes
_____ 11. goods whose demand falls as consumer income increases	c. *ceteris paribus*
_____ 12. goods that are bought and used together	d. inferior goods
_____ 13. goods that are used in place of one another	e. complements

Section 3: Guided Reading and Review
Elasticity of Demand

A. As You Read
As you read Section 3, supply the missing information in the spaces provided.

Calculating Elasticity (Provide a formula or numerical value.)

1. Computation of elasticity of demand: _____

   _____

2. Elastic demand: _____

   _____

3. Inelastic demand: _____

   _____

4. Unitary elastic demand: _____

   _____

Factors Affecting Elasticity (How does each affect elasticity?)

5. Substitutes: _____

   _____

6. Necessities vs. luxuries: _____

   _____

7. Changes over time: _____

   _____

Elasticity and Revenue (Define and explain.)

8. Total revenue: _____

   _____

9. How elasticity affects a company's pricing: _____

   _____

B. Reviewing Key Terms
Briefly define or identify each of the following.

10. elasticity of demand _____

11. inelastic _____

12. elastic _____

13. unitary elastic _____

Section 1: Guided Reading and Review
Understanding Supply

A. As You Read

As you read Section 1, supply the missing causes or effects on the lines provided in the chart.

Cause	Effect
1. The price of pizza increases.	1. *On pizzerias:* _____ _____
2. The cost of tomato sauce increases along with the price of pizza.	2. *On pizza supply schedule:* _____ _____
3. _____ _____ _____ _____	3. *On market supply curve:* Prices will remain the same as on a single pizzeria's supply curve.
4. _____ _____ _____ _____	4. *On supply curve:* The curve always rises from left to right.
5. The supply of a good is not very responsive to price changes.	5. *On the value of elasticity of supply:* _____ _____
6. A supplier, such as an orange grower, has a long time to respond to a price change.	6. *On supply:* _____ _____

B. Reviewing Key Terms

Read the statements below. In the space provided, write *T* if the statement is true or *F* if it is false.

_____ 7. Price and quantity supplied are variables on a supply schedule.

_____ 8. A supply curve shows price and quantity in a table.

_____ 9. Elasticity of supply states that the output of a good increases as the price of the good increases.

_____ 10. To create a market supply schedule, an economist needs to know the total output of all suppliers in a given market.

Section 2: Guided Reading and Review
Costs of Production

A. As You Read
As you read Section 2, supply the requested information in the spaces provided.

1. A basic question a producer must answer: _____

   _____

2. Marginal product of labor benefits gained from worker specialization: _____

   _____

3. Negative effect of a firm's limited capital: _____

   _____

4. Curve pattern for marginal product of labor when capital is limited: _____

   _____

   _____

5. Examples of typical fixed costs: _____

   _____

   _____

6. Why labor is a variable cost: _____

   _____

7. How the marginal costs of production for the beanbag producer changed after the rate of
   three bags per hour was surpassed: _____

   _____

   _____

8. How total revenue and total cost can help set the most profitable output level: _____

   _____

9. How marginal revenue and marginal cost can help set the most profitable output level:

   _____

10. Why a producer would continue to increase output even though the marginal cost of pro-
    duction may be rising: _____

    _____

B. Reviewing Key Terms
Define the following terms.

11. marginal product of labor _____

12. diminishing marginal returns _____

13. total cost _____

14. marginal cost _____

Section 3: Guided Reading and Review
Changes in Supply

A. As You Read
As you read Section 3, supply information to complete each statement in the spaces provided.

1. Unable to control price, a profitable producer faced with rising labor and/or materials costs will

   _____.

2. New technology affects supply by

   _____.

3. European governments' reasons for subsidizing food producers include

   _____.

4. In the past, Western European governments subsidized banks and airlines by

   _____.

5. The United States government subsidizes such industries as

   _____

   _____.

6. An excise tax increases production costs by

   _____

   _____.

7. Consumers may be unaware of excise taxes because

   _____

   _____.

8. Government regulations often reduce supply because

   _____

   _____.

9. During periods of inflation, suppliers may temporarily withhold goods that can be stored
   for long periods because

   _____

   _____.

B. Reviewing Key Terms
Complete each sentence by writing the correct key term in the blank provided.

10. Government can increase supply by granting producers a(n) _____.

11. To reduce supply, a government might levy a(n) _____.

12. Requiring pollution control on automobiles exemplifies government

    _____.

Section 1: Guided Reading and Review
Combining Supply and Demand

A. As You Read
As you read Section 1, supply the requested information in the spaces provided.

In the Case of the Pizzerias

1. The market equilibrium price: _____

2. The market supply level: _____

3. The market demand level: _____

In Any Market Environment

4. How equilibrium is shown on a supply and demand graph: _____
   _____

5. Two possible outcomes of disequilibrium: _____
   _____

6. Supplier price response to excess demand: _____
   _____

7. Condition under which market forces will push market toward the equilibrium: _____
   _____

In the Case of Government Intervention

8. Purpose(s) of rent control: _____
   _____

9. Negative results of ending rent control: _____
   _____

10. Effect on labor when minimum wage exceeds equilibrium: _____

11. Purpose of Northeast Dairy Compact: _____
    _____

B. Reviewing Key Terms
Complete each sentence by writing the correct term in the blank provided.

12. When government wants to ensure that "essential" goods or services are within the reach of all consumers, it may impose a(n) _____.

13. If prices rise too high, a market may face the problem of _____.

14. The one and only price at which quantities supplied equal quantities demanded indicates the market _____.

15. Minimum wage is an example of a government-imposed _____.

16. If car manufacturers produce more or fewer cars than customers will buy, the car market will be in _____.

Section 2: Guided Reading and Review
Changes in Market Equilibrium

A. As You Read
As you read Section 2, complete the chart by supplying an effect for each cause.

Cause	Effect
1. Entire supply curve shifts.	1.
2. Technology for making compact disc (CD) players improved.	2.
3. After a drop in production cost, CD player suppliers become willing to offer 1,200,000 units at the original price, but demand remains at 1,000,000.	3.
4. Price of CD players continues to fall.	4.
5. Production cost of CD players continues to fall.	5.
6. Market's supply curve shifts to the left.	6. *In the market:* *On the equilibrium point:*
7. Demand curve of a good suddenly shifts right.	7.
8. Signs of excess demand for the good continue over time.	8. *On suppliers:*
9. Demand for a good falls.	9. *On the demand curve:*

B. Reviewing Key Terms
Rewrite each sentence so that the italicized term is used correctly.

10. *Shortage* occurs when the quantity demanded falls below the quantity supplied.

    _____

    _____

11. Excess demand for a good indicates a market *surplus* of that good.

    _____

    _____

12. Suppliers pay *search costs* in the form of financial and opportunity costs as they search for a good.

    _____

    _____

Section 3: Guided Reading and Review
The Role of Prices

A. As You Read

As you read Section 3, answer the questions on the lines provided.

1. What overall, vital role do prices play in the free market? _____
_____
_____

2. What standard do prices set? _____

3. What signals do high prices send to producers and consumers? _____
_____

4. Why do suppliers use price rather than production to resolve the problem of excess
demand? _____
_____

5. What drives the distribution system in the free market? _____
_____

6. How does a price-driven economy allow for a wide diversity of goods? _____
_____

7. What was the goal of the Soviet planned economy? _____
_____

8. How did the Soviet economic system affect consumer goods? _____
_____

9. How does the free market ensure an efficient allocation of resources? _____
_____
_____

10. What motivates suppliers to increase production in the face of high demand and high
prices? _____
_____

11. What three problems in the free market work against the efficient allocation of resources?
_____

B. Reviewing Key Terms

Define the following terms.

12. supply shock _____

13. rationing _____

14. spillover costs _____
_____

Section 1: Guided Reading and Review
Perfect Competition

A. As You Read
As you read Section 1, supply the missing cause or effect in the spaces provided.

The Perfect Market Structure	
1. Cause: _____ _____	1. **Effect:** The market determines price without influence from suppliers or consumers.
2. Cause: _____ _____	2. **Effect:** Identical products are key to perfect competition.
3. Cause: Entrepreneurs are less likely to enter a market with high start-up costs.	3. **Effect:** _____ _____
4. Cause: Sometimes firms cannot make enough to stay in business.	4. **Effect:** _____ _____
5. Cause: _____ _____	5. **Effect:** Prices are forced down to the point where they just cover the seller's costs of doing business.
6. Cause: _____ _____	6. **Effect:** Producers adjust their output decisions based on their most efficient use of available land, labor, and capital.

B. Reviewing Key Terms
Briefly define or identify each of the following.

7. perfect competition _____

_____

_____

8. commodity _____

_____

_____

9. barrier to entry _____

_____

_____

10. start-up costs _____

_____

_____

Section 2: Guided Reading and Review
Monopoly

A. As You Read
As you read Section 2, supply the missing information in the spaces provided.

In the Monopolist Market

Natural Monopolies

1. Why they exist _____
   _____

2. Two examples _____
   _____

3. Advantage of _____
   _____

4. Government role in _____
   _____

Government Monopolies

5. Type set up by patents
   _____

6. Why government grants patented monopolies
   _____

7. Example of an industrial monopoly
   _____

8. Two examples of government monopolies by license
   _____

Production and Pricing

9. Effect of a monopolist's price increase
   _____
   _____

10. Relationship between price and marginal revenue when a monopolist cuts the price to sell more
    _____
    _____

11. How a monopolist maximizes profits
    _____
    _____

B. Reviewing Key Terms
Complete each sentence by writing the correct key term in the blank.

12. In a market with only one seller, that seller has a _____.

13. Characteristics that cause a producer's average cost to drop as production rises are _____.

14. A contract issued by a local authority that gives a single firm the right to sell its goods within an exclusive market is a _____.

15. A monopoly offering targeted discounts is practicing _____.

Section 3: Guided Reading and Review
Monopolistic Competition and Oligopoly

A. As You Read

As you read Section 3, fill in the information requested on the charts.

Monopolistic Competition Market Structures		
Defining Conditions	1. _____ 3. _____	2. _____ 4. _____
Forms of Nonprice Competition	5. _____ 7. _____	6. _____ 8. _____
Price-Output Relationship	9. _____	
Curbs on High Profits	10. _____	11. _____
Consumer Advantages	12. _____	
Oligopoly		
Conditions Encouraging Formation	13. _____ 15. _____	14. _____
Practices that Concern Government	16. _____ 18. _____	17. _____

B. Reviewing Key Terms

Read the statements below. In the space provided, write T if the statement is true or F if it is false.

_____ **19.** Firms selling identical products create *monopolistic competition.*

_____ **20.** Providing better customer service, introducing a new lipstick color, and sophisticated advertising are examples of *nonprice competition.*

_____ **21.** *Price fixing* is an outcome of collusion.

_____ **22.** A *cartel* is most successful when each member produces as much product as possible.

Section 4: Guided Reading and Review
Regulation and Deregulation

A. As You Read

As you read Section 4, supply the missing information about government market intervention in the numbered web boxes.

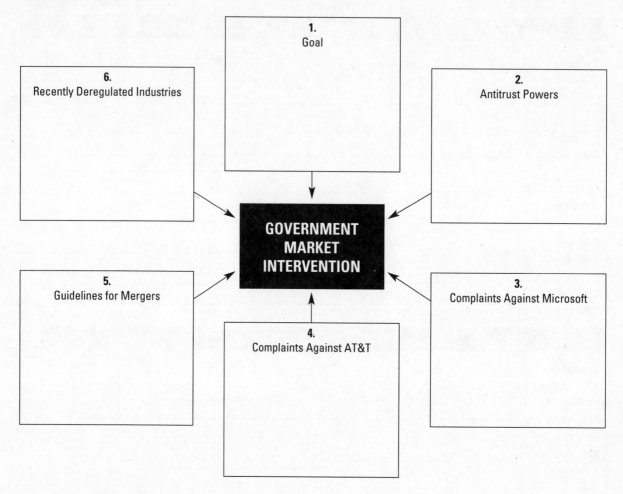

1.
Goal

6.
Recently Deregulated Industries

2.
Antitrust Powers

GOVERNMENT MARKET INTERVENTION

5.
Guidelines for Mergers

3.
Complaints Against Microsoft

4.
Complaints Against AT&T

B. Reviewing Key Terms

Use a key term to rewrite each sentence correctly.

7. *Price fixing* is the practice of setting the market price below cost for the short term to drive competitors out of business. _____

_____

8. A *monopoly* occurs when a company joins with another company to form a single firm.

_____

_____

9. *Perfect competition* means that the government no longer decides a company's market role and pricing. _____

_____

Section 1: Guided Reading and Review
Sole Proprietorships

A. As You Read
As you read Section 1, supply the missing information in the spaces provided.

Sole Proprietorships

1. Owned and managed by: _____

2. Percentage of U.S. businesses: _____

3. Percentages of U.S. sales generated: _____

List and explain the advantages of sole proprietorships.

4. _____

5. _____

6. _____

7. _____

8. _____

List and explain the disadvantages of sole proprietorships.

9. _____

10. _____

11. _____

B. Reviewing Key Terms
Find the term that does not belong in each set and explain how it does not relate to the other three.

12. (*business license*, certificate of occupancy, *business organization*, registration of business name) _____

_____

_____

13. (*liability*, health codes, *zoning laws*, dangerous chemical codes)

_____

_____

_____

14. (human capital, *fringe benefits*, physical capital, financial resources)

_____

_____

_____

Section 2: Guided Reading and Review
Partnerships

A. As You Read
As you read Section 2, supply the requested information in the spaces provided.

1. Typical examples of a general partnership

    1. _____

      _____

      _____

2. What limited partners do and do not do

    2. _____

      _____

      _____

3. How limited liability partnerships compare with general partnerships

    3. _____

      _____

      _____

4. Items often covered under articles of partnership

    4. _____

      _____

      _____

5. Capital and taxation advantages of partnerships

    5. _____

      _____

      _____

6. Liability disadvantages of partnerships

    6. _____

      _____

      _____

B. Reviewing Key Terms
Complete each sentence by writing the correct term in the blank.

7. Only one partner is required to be a general partner in a _____.

8. Money and other valuables make up a person's or firm's _____.

9. Ownership interests and management responsibilities are legislated under the _____.

Section 3: Guided Reading and Review
Corporations, Mergers, and Multinationals

A. As You Read
As you read Section 3, supply the missing information in the graphic organizer.

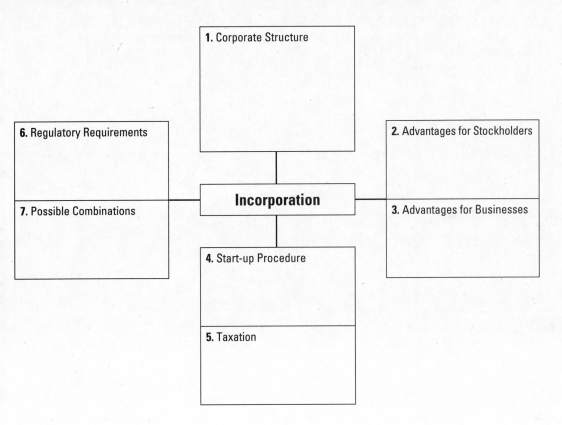

1. Corporate Structure

6. Regulatory Requirements

7. Possible Combinations

Incorporation

2. Advantages for Stockholders

3. Advantages for Businesses

4. Start-up Procedure

5. Taxation

B. Reviewing Key Terms
Read the statements below. In the space provided, write *T* if the statement is true, or *F* if it is false.

____ **8.** Companies in the same business might form vertical mergers.

____ **9.** Multinational corporations usually headquarter in several countries.

____ **10.** If you buy stocks, you own part of a corporation.

____ **11.** Corporate bonds pay dividends.

____ **12.** Corporations have a legal identity.

____ **13.** Dividends represent a portion of corporate profits.

____ **14.** Privately held corporations are also closely held corporations.

____ **15.** The federal government issues a company's certificate of incorporation.

____ **16.** A conglomerate merges more than three companies making unrelated products.

____ **17.** Publicly held corporations sell stocks to the Securities and Exchange Commission.

____ **18.** Stockholders must pay a capital gains tax whenever they sell their shares.

Section 4: Guided Reading and Review
Other Organizations

A. As You Read

As you read Section 4, supply the missing information under the headings on the chart.

Business Franchises

Advantages	Disadvantages
1.	2.

Cooperative Organizations

Membership and/or Purpose	Categories
3.	4.

Nonprofit Organizations

5.	6.

B. Reviewing Key Terms

Briefly define or identify each of the following.

7. royalties _____

_____

_____

8. trade association _____

_____

_____

9. cooperative _____

_____

_____

Section 1: Guided Reading and Review
Labor Market Trends

A. As You Read

As you read Section 1, fill in two supporting facts or details under each main idea by answering each question.

Main Idea: The Bureau of Labor Statistics (BLS) tracks changes in the labor force.

1. How do economists define *labor force*? _____

   _____

2. What criteria define unemployment? _____

   _____

Main Idea: The changing economy has brought along a changing job market.

3. How did the electronics boom of the mid-twentieth century impact the job market?

   _____

4. What new jobs were created beginning in the 1970s? _____

   _____

Main Idea: Changes in the labor force can be traced to a number of causes.

5. How has higher education contributed? _____

   _____

6. Why are there more women in the labor force? _____

   _____

Main Idea: For about the past 20 years, the trend in average wage earnings can be described as slightly downward.

7. Have all workers received lower wages? _____

   _____

8. How has competition affected wage earnings? _____

   _____

B. Reviewing Key Terms

Answer each of the following questions in a complete sentence.

9. How might the *learning effect* influence wage trends? _____

10. According to the *screening effect*, how may employers view job applicants who have a college education? _____

11. To what kinds of jobs does *contingent employment* refer? _____

Section 2: Guided Reading and Review
Labor and Wages

A. As You Read

As you read Section 2, complete each of the following sentences.

1. Employment in a labor market depends on how closely the demand for workers meets _____.

2. The price of labor (earnings) depends on _____.

3. Professional labor requires _____.

4. In a competitive market, workers are usually paid according to _____.

5. Higher labor prices decrease the _____.

6. Firms can respond to higher wages by replacing _____.

7. Higher wages increase the _____.

8. Jobs in the skilled labor category require _____.

9. A high equilibrium wage is the result of _____.

10. The Equal Pay Act of 1963 provided that _____.

11. Title VII of the 1964 Civil Rights Act forbids job discrimination on the basis of _____.

12. Lack of human capital and possible discrimination contribute to low wages for _____.

13. Negative effects on nonunion wages can be reduced when unions _____.

B. Reviewing Key Terms

Define the following terms.

14. labor force _____

_____

_____

15. equilibrium wage _____

_____

_____

16. glass ceiling _____

_____

_____

17. featherbedding _____

_____

_____

Section 3: Guided Reading and Review
Organized Labor

A. As You Read

As you read Section 3, supply the information requested by the heading in each box.

Economic changes that have affected unions:

9. _____

10. _____

11. _____

Major U.S. labor organizations formed between 1869 and 1955:

1. *(1869)* _____

2. *(1886)* _____

3. *(1938)* _____

4. *(1955)* _____

Ways in which unions have declined in traditional strongholds:

12. _____

13. _____

14. _____

15. _____

Anti-union strategies used by U.S. employers before the 1930s:

5. _____

6. _____

7. _____

8. _____

Major issues covered under a union contract:

16. _____

17. _____

18. _____

B. Reviewing Key Terms

Match the definitions in Column I with the terms in Column II. Write the letter of the correct answer in the blank provided. You will not use all of the terms.

Column I

_____ 19. union and company representatives meeting to negotiate a contract

_____ 20. worker in a professional job receiving a salary

_____ 21. measure banning mandatory union membership

_____ 22. worker in an industrial job

_____ 23. settlement technique using third party reviews

_____ 24. organized work stoppage

Column II

a. arbitration

b. strike

c. blue-collar worker

d. collective bargaining

e. white-collar worker

f. mediation

g. right-to-work law

Section 1: Guided Reading and Review
Money

A. As You Read

As you read Section 1, supply the requested information in the spaces provided.

Describe the three uses of money.

1. _____

2. _____

3. _____

Define the six characteristics of money.

4. _____

5. _____

6. _____

7. _____

8. _____

9. _____

B. Reviewing Key Terms

Match the definitions in Column I with the terms in Column II. Write the letter of the correct answer in the blank provided.

Column I

_____ 10. something that keeps its value if held

_____ 11. objects that have value because the holder can exchange them for something else of value

_____ 12. money that has value because the government says it is acceptable for paying debts

_____ 13. anything that is used to determine value during the exchange of goods and services

_____ 14. exchange of one set of goods or services for another

_____ 15. coins and paper bills used as money

_____ 16. way to compare the value of goods and services relative to each other

_____ 17. anything used as a medium of exchange, a unit of account, and a store of value

_____ 18. objects that have value in themselves as well as for their use as money

Column II

a. barter

b. store of value

c. fiat money

d. currency

e. money

f. medium of exchange

g. commodity money

h. unit of account

i. representative money

Section 2: Guided Reading and Review
The History of American Banking

A. As You Read

As you read Section 2, fill in two supporting facts or details under each main idea by answering each question.

Main Idea: Before the Civil War, banking in the United States shifted between a centralized system and independent state and local banks.

1. What were the first two attempts to centralize U.S. banking, and when were they in operation? _____

   _____

2. What problems were associated with the Free Banking Era (1837–1863), dominated by state-chartered banks? _____

   _____

Main Idea: Reforms of the late 1800s stabilized the banking system.

3. How did the National Banking Acts of 1863 and 1864 promote stability? _____

   _____

4. How did the gold standard promote stability? _____

   _____

Main Idea: Banking reforms early in the twentieth century helped strengthen and centralize American banking.

5. How did the Federal Reserve System, established in 1913, begin to manage the money supply? _____

   _____

6. What guarantee was made available to bank customers in 1933? _____

   _____

B. Reviewing Key Terms

Complete each sentence by writing the correct term in the blank provided.

7. One advantage of the _____ was that the government could only issue currency if it had gold in the treasury to back it.

8. The _____ was a paper currency printed with green ink that was issued by the U.S. Treasury during the Civil War but not backed by gold or silver.

9. A(n) _____ receives, keeps, and lends money.

10. The nation's central banking system is the _____.

Section 3: Guided Reading and Review
Banking Today

A. As You Read

As you read Section 3, supply the requested information on the lines provided.

Define M1.

1. _____

_____

Define M2.

2. _____

_____

List five services that banks offer.

3. _____

4. _____

5. _____

6. _____

7. _____

Describe four types of financial institutions.

8. _____

9. _____

10. _____

11. _____

B. Reviewing Key Terms

Define the following terms.

12. money supply _____

13. liquidity _____

14. demand deposit _____

15. money market mutual fund _____

16. fractional reserve banking _____

17. default _____

18. mortgage _____

19. credit card _____

20. interest _____

21. debit card _____

22. creditor _____

Section 1: Guided Reading and Review
Saving and Investing

A. As You Read

As you read Section 1, supply the missing information about the functions of the financial intermediaries in the chart below.

Financial Intermediaries	Functions
1. Banks, Savings and Loan Associations, Credit Unions	1.
2. Finance Companies	2.
3. Mutual Funds	3.
4. Life Insurance Companies	4.
5. Pension Funds	5.

B. Reviewing Key Terms

Complete each sentence by writing the correct key term in the blank provided.

6. Before putting money into mutual funds, a potential investor can review the fund's performance in its _____.

7. The use of assets to earn income or profit constitutes a(n) _____.

8. To transfer money between savers and borrowers, allowing investment to take place, an economy needs a(n) _____.

9. Securities is another name for _____.

10. The lower the risk in an investment, the lower its _____.

11. The collection of all one's financial assets makes up one's _____.

Section 2: Guided Reading and Review
Bonds and Other Financial Assets

A. As You Read
As you read Section 2, answer the questions on the lines provided.

1. How does an investor earn money by buying bonds at a discount? _____
   _____
   _____

2. What are Standard & Poor's and Moody's ratings based on? _____
   _____
   _____

3. What advantages do bonds offer to firms that issue them? _____
   _____
   _____

4. What disadvantage do bonds present for the issuer? _____
   _____
   _____

5. (a) What types of government bonds are available to investors? _____
   _____

   (b) Which type offers the greatest tax advantage? _____
   _____

6. What three organizations help ensure value and prevent dishonesty in the bond market?
   _____

7. (a) What is the investment advantage of money market mutual funds over CDs and savings
   accounts? _____
   (b) What is the disadvantage? _____

8. (a) In financial asset markets, how do capital markets differ from money markets? _____
   _____

   (b) How do primary markets differ from secondary markets? _____
   _____

B. Reviewing Key Terms
Define the following terms.

9. maturity _____

10. corporate bond _____

11. junk bond _____

12. coupon rate _____

NAME _____ CLASS _____ DATE _____

A. As You Read

As you read Section 3, supply the missing information to complete each sentence in the spaces provided.

1. Income stocks pay _____.

2. Growth stocks can be profitable because they _____.

3. Investors experience capital gains when they _____

_____.

4. Investors suffer capital losses when they _____

_____.

5. Stocks are riskier than bonds because _____

_____

_____.

6. Blue chip stocks are traded on the _____

7. A put option is the option to _____

_____.

8. During a bear market, investors sell because _____

_____.

B. Reviewing Key Terms

Match the descriptions in Column I with the terms in Column II. Write the letter of the correct answer in the blank provided. You will not use all the terms.

Column I

_____ 9. steady, extended rise in stock market

_____ 10. electronic marketplace for stock not listed on an organized exchange

_____ 11. claims of ownership in a corporation

_____ 12. making high-risk investments with borrowed money in the hope of getting a big return

_____ 13. market for buying and selling stock

_____ 14. person who links buyers and sellers of stocks

_____ 15. 1929 collapse of the stock market

_____ 16. business specializing in trading stocks

_____ 17. contracts to trade stock at a specific price and time in the future

Column II

a. stockbroker

b. options

c. bear market

d. Great Crash

e. brokerage firm

f. bull market

g. equities

h. OTC market

i. speculation

j. stock exchange

Section 1: Guided Reading and Review
Gross Domestic Product

A. As You Read
As you read Section 1, answer the following questions about gross domestic product.

1. What is the gross domestic product? _____

2. How is the expenditure approach used to calculate it? _____

3. How is the income approach used to calculate it? _____

4. What is the difference between nominal GDP and real GDP? _____

Describe four limitations of using GDP to measure economic growth:

5. _____

6. _____

7. _____

8. _____

9. How is the gross national product derived from the gross domestic product? _____

10. How is GDP related to aggregate supply and aggregate demand? _____

B. Reviewing Key Terms
Match the descriptions in Column I with the terms in Column II. Write the letter of the correct answer in the blank provided. You will not use all the terms.

Column I

_____ 11. a system that collects macroeconomic statistics on production, income, investment, and savings

_____ 12. goods used in the production of final goods

_____ 13. GDP measured in current prices

_____ 14. goods that last a short period of time

_____ 15. GDP expressed in constant, or unchanging, prices

_____ 16. goods that last for a relatively long time

_____ 17. loss of the value of capital equipment that results from normal wear and tear

_____ 18. the total amount of goods and services in the economy available at all possible price levels

_____ 19. the average of all prices in the economy

_____ 20. the annual income earned by U.S.-owned firms and U.S. residents

_____ 21. the dollar value of all final goods and services produced within a country's borders in a given year

Column II

a. real GDP

b. nominal GDP

c. aggregate supply

d. nondurable goods

e. price level

f. intermediate goods

g. depreciation

h. national income accounting

i. gross domestic product

j. durable goods

k. gross national product

l. aggregate demand

NAME _____ CLASS _____ DATE _____

Section 2: Guided Reading and Review
Business Cycles

A. As You Read
As you read Section 2, fill in each item in the following diagram.

BUSINESS CYCLE		
Phases	**Contributing Factors**	**Cycle Indicators**
1. _____	5. _____	9. _____
2. _____	6. _____	10. _____
3. _____	7. _____	11. _____
4. _____	8. _____	

B. Reviewing Key Terms
Define the following terms.

12. business cycle _____

13. expansion _____

14. economic growth _____

15. peak _____

16. contraction _____

17. trough _____

18. recession _____

19. depression _____

20. stagflation _____

21. leading indicators _____

Section 3: Guided Reading and Review
Economic Growth

A. As You Read
As you read Section 3, fill in supporting facts or details under each main idea by answering each question.

Main Idea: Capital deepening is an important source of growth in modern economies.

1. How does capital deepening increase output per worker? _____

   _____

2. How is human capital deepened? _____

   _____

Main Idea: The rate of saving and investment affects the economy.

3. What happens when saving rises? _____

   _____

4. How does increased investment help the economy? _____

   _____

Main Idea: Population, government, and trade all directly affect the economy.

5. What happens when population grows and capital remains constant? _____

   _____

6. How do government taxation for consumption spending and importing goods for short-term consumption affect economic growth? _____

   _____

Main Idea: Technological progress is a key source of economic growth.

7. How do economists measure the impact of technological progress on economic growth?

   _____

8. How does the government aid technological innovation? _____

   _____

B. Reviewing Key Terms
Complete each sentence by writing the correct term in the blank.

9. _____ is the proportion of disposable income spent to income saved.

10. The real GDP divided by the total population is called _____.

11. Increasing the amount of capital per worker is _____.

12. Income not used for consumption is considered _____.

13. An increase in efficiency gained by producing more output without using more inputs is called _____.

Section 1: Guided Reading and Review
Unemployment

A. As You Read

As you read Section 1, supply the missing reason for or type of unemployment on the lines provided in the chart.

Reason for Unemployment	Type of Unemployment
1. people taking time looking for work after finishing school	1. _____
2. _____	2. structural unemployment
3. lack of education or training for skills in demand	3. _____
4. _____	4. frictional unemployment
5. a healthy economy that is working properly	5. _____
6. _____	6. seasonal unemployment
7. _____	7. very low unemployment
8. _____	8. structural unemployment
9. development of new technologies	9. _____
10. _____	10. cyclical unemployment
11. _____	11. structural unemployment

B. Reviewing Key Terms

Complete each sentence by writing the correct term in the blank provided.

12. My cousin Harold is used to _____, since he works for a landscaping company and is laid off every winter.

13. It is easy to find a job these days, since the _____ is so low.

14. People who do not finish high school often suffer from _____.

15. With _____, nearly everyone who wants a job has a job.

16. The excellent mechanic who has been working as a clerk at a convenience store since the local garage closed is considered _____.

17. My aunt who left her job to care for her sick mother and is now looking for work is an example of _____.

Section 2: Guided Reading and Review
Inflation

A. As You Read

As you read Section 2, answer the following questions.

1. What would you use to see how prices have changed over time? _____

   _____

2. What does the example of the Barrow's house increasing from $12,000 to $150,000 over 50 years show? _____

   _____

3. How is the Consumer Price Index (CPI) used? _____

   _____

4. How does the Bureau of Labor Statistics determine the CPI? _____

   _____

   _____

5. What data must you have to calculate the inflation rate for a specific year? _____

   _____

6. What happens when hyperinflation occurs over an extended period of time? _____

   _____

Describe three theories of the causes of inflation.

7. _____

8. _____

9. _____

How does inflation affect each of the following?

10. purchasing power _____

11. fixed income _____

12. savings _____

B. Reviewing Key Terms

Define the following terms.

13. inflation rate _____

14. deflation _____

15. Consumer Price Index _____

16. inflation _____

17. wage-price spiral _____

18. price index _____

Section 3: Guided Reading and Review
Poverty

A. As You Read

As you read Section 3, fill in two supporting facts or details under each main idea by answering each question.

Main Idea: The U.S. Census Bureau has developed measurements to calculate the number of poor.

1. What condition must exist for everyone in a household to be counted as poor? _____

   _____

2. What does the poverty rate help us understand? _____

   _____

Main Idea: Poverty has a number of root causes.

3. What do statistics show about a lack of education contributing to poverty? _____

   _____

4. What has the divorce rate shown about poverty? _____

   _____

Main Idea: Knowing how the nation's total income is distributed helps people understand poverty.

5. What percentage of the nation's total income does the lowest 40 percent of the population receive? _____

   _____

6. What two key factors contribute to the differences in income distribution? _____

   _____

Main Idea: The government has various programs and policies to combat poverty.

7. What programs and laws help working people achieve an adequate income? _____

   _____

8. How might the welfare reform program help reduce poverty? _____

   _____

B. Reviewing Key Terms

Complete each sentence by writing the correct term in the blank.

9. The _____ is the graphed curve that illustrates income distribution in the economy.

10. The program that requires work in exchange for assistance is called _____.

11. The _____ is the percentage of people in a particular group who are officially considered living in poverty.

12. The level of income below which income is insufficient to support a family or household is called the _____.

Section 1: Guided Reading and Review
What Are Taxes?

A. As You Read

As you read Section 1, supply the requested information in the spaces provided.
Explain what gives the government the power to collect taxes.

1. _____

List four ways in which the government's power to tax is limited.

2. _____

3. _____

4. _____

5. _____

List and define the three types of tax structures.

6. _____

7. _____

8. _____

List and define the characteristics of a good tax.

9. _____
_____

10. _____
_____

11. _____
_____

12. _____
_____

B. Reviewing Key Terms

Complete each sentence by writing the correct term in the blank provided.

13. The income, property, good, or service that is subject to tax is considered a

_____ .

14. The _____ is the final burden of a tax.

15. Sales tax is a type of _____ tax.

16. With a _____ the percentage of income paid in taxes remains the same for all income levels.

17. Income tax is a type of _____ tax.

18. The income that government receives is called _____ .

Section 2: Guided Reading and Review
Federal Taxes

A. As You Read

As you read Section 2, fill in supporting facts or details under each main idea by answering each question.

Main Idea: Individual income taxes are imposed on the income of all individuals living in the country.

1. Why do employers withhold a set amount of your income? _____
_____

2. What is taxable income? _____
_____

Main Idea: Federal Insurance Contributions Act (FICA) taxes fund two large government programs.

3. What does Social Security provide? _____
_____
_____

4. What is Medicare? _____
_____
_____

Main Idea: Taxes are sometimes used to affect behavior.

5. What items are taxed for the purpose of changing behavior? _____
_____
_____

B. Reviewing Key Terms

Match the descriptions in Column I with the terms in Column II. Write the letter of the correct answer in the blank provided.

Column I

_____ 6. amounts that you can subtract from your income when filing taxes

_____ 7. form used to file one's income taxes

_____ 8. income on which tax must be paid

_____ 9. tax on a monetary gift from a living person valued above a certain amount

_____ 10. tax on the total value of the money and property of a person who has died

_____ 11. tax payments taken out of an employee's pay before he or she receives a paycheck

_____ 12. tax levied on foreign goods brought into the United States

Column II

a. taxable income

b. tariff

c. tax return

d. withholding

e. deductions

f. gift tax

g. estate tax

Section 3: Guided Reading and Review
Federal Spending

A. As You Read

As you read Section 3, provide examples of the categories of federal spending in the diagram below.

Categories of Federal Spending

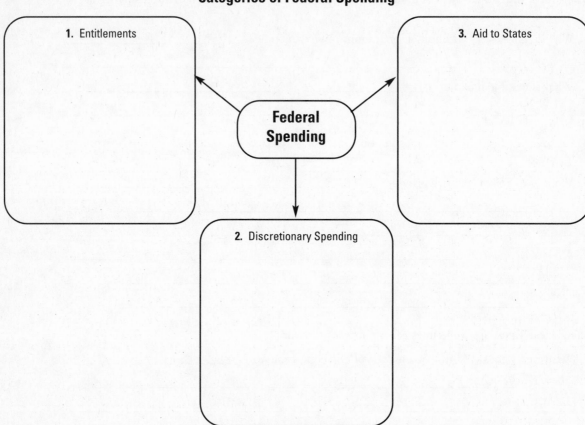

1. Entitlements

Federal Spending

3. Aid to States

2. Discretionary Spending

B. Reviewing Key Terms

Define the following terms.

4. discretionary spending _____

_____

5. mandatory spending _____

_____

6. entitlement _____

_____

NAME _____ CLASS _____ DATE _____

Section 4: Guided Reading and Review
State and Local Taxes and Spending

A. As You Read
As you read Section 4, fill in examples of each item in the space provided.

Spending

(State Governments)

Provide examples of goods or services on which state taxes are spent for each category.

1. Education: _____
   _____

2. Public Safety: _____
   _____

3. Highways and Transportation: _____
   _____

4. General Welfare: _____
   _____

5. Arts and Recreation: _____
   _____

6. Administration: _____
   _____

Sources of Revenue

(State Governments)

Provide examples of each type of tax from which states earn revenue.

7. Sales Tax: _____
   _____

8. Excise Tax: _____
   _____

9. Income Tax: _____
   _____

10. Corporate Income Tax: _____
    _____

11. Business Taxes: _____
    _____

(Local Governments)

Provide examples of goods or services on which local taxes are spent for each category.

12. Law enforcement: _____
    _____

13. Public facilities: _____
    _____

14. Public health: _____
    _____

(Local Governments)

Provide examples of each type of tax from which local governments earn revenue.

15. Property Taxes: _____
    _____

16. Other Taxes: _____
    _____

B. Reviewing Key Terms
Answer each of the following questions.

17. What is the difference between real property and personal property? _____
    _____

18. What is the difference between an operating budget and a capital budget? _____
    _____

19. What is a sales tax? _____
    _____

20. What is the relationship between revenues and spending in a balanced budget? _____
    _____

Section 1: Guided Reading and Review
Understanding Fiscal Policy

A. As You Read

As you read Section 1, fill in two supporting facts or details under each main idea by answering each question.

Main Idea: The president and Congress work through a budget process to draw up a spending plan for the following fiscal year.

1. Which part of the executive branch is responsible for preparing the president's budget proposal? _____

2. Which congressional committees submit the final bills that authorize specific spending?

_____

Main Idea: The federal government may use fiscal policy to try to make the economy run more smoothly.

3. Under what conditions might the government use expansionary fiscal policies? _____

_____

4. Under what conditions might the government use contractionary fiscal policies? _____

_____

Main Idea: The federal government has specific policies that it uses to influence the economy.

5. What are its two main expansionary policies? _____

_____

6. What are its two main contractionary policies? _____

_____

Main Idea: Although fiscal policies may appear to be powerful economic tools, they can be difficult to put into practice.

7. What kinds of entitlement programs make it difficult to change spending levels? _____

_____

8. Why does it take so long to put fiscal changes into effect? _____

_____

B. Reviewing Key Terms

Answer each of the following questions.

9. What is the federal budget? _____

10. What is the main function of the Congressional Budget Office? _____

11. What is the overall goal of expansionary policies? _____

12. What is the overall goal of contractionary policies? _____

Guided Reading and Review

Section 2: Guided Reading and Review
Fiscal Policy Options

A. As You Read
As you read Section 2, answer the following questions.

1. What failure of classical economics did the Great Depression highlight? _____
   _____

2. How did John Maynard Keynes explain the continuation of the Great Depression? _____
   _____

3. (a) According to Keynes, how could the Depression-era government make up for the drop
   in private spending? _____

   (b) What did Keynes say the result would be? _____

4. (a) What economic data did Keynes say the federal government should track? _____
   _____

   (b) For what purpose? _____
   _____

5. Why did Keynesian economics lose popularity in the 1960s and 1970s? _____
   _____

6. What is a stable economy? _____

7. When national income is low, how do taxes and government transfer payments help stabi-
   lize the economy? _____
   _____

8. According to supply-side economics and the Laffer curve, how do higher tax rates affect
   the economy? _____
   _____

9. What argument lies at the heart of supply-side economics? _____
   _____

10. How did President Kennedy propose to increase demand? _____

B. Reviewing Key Terms
Use a key term to complete each sentence.

11. An economy sustains maximum output for a period of time when it operates at

    _____.

12. The idea that in a free market, people act in their own self-interest, causing prices to rise or
    fall so that supply and demand will always return to equilibrium is the thinking in

    _____.

13. Taxes and transfer payments act as _____.

14. The idea that every dollar change in fiscal policy creates a greater than one dollar change in
    the economy explains the _____.

Section 3: Guided Reading and Review
Budget Deficits and the National Debt

A. As You Read
As you read Section 3, complete the following sentences.

1. When the government increases the amount of money in circulation to cover large deficits, inflation results because _____

   _____

   _____.

2. Wise federal borrowing allows the government to _____

   _____

   _____.

3. The national debt will grow each year that _____

   _____.

4. The national debt is owned by _____

   _____

   _____.

5. Historically, national debt as a percentage of GDP rises during _____

   _____.

6. The two problems of a national debt are that _____

   _____

   _____.

7. The opportunity cost of servicing the debt is that _____

   _____

   _____.

8. Today, many economists think the role of the federal government in the economy should be

   _____.

B. Reviewing Key Terms
Define the following terms.

9. budget surplus _____

   _____

10. hyperinflation _____

    _____

11. national debt _____

12. Treasury bill _____

    _____

Section 1: Guided Reading and Review
The Federal Reserve System

A. As You Read

As you read Section 1, supply the requested information.

1. Sources of confusion and problems with American banking between 1836 and 1907:

   _____

   _____

2. Why the Federal Reserve System was unable to hold off the Great Depression: _____

   _____

   _____

3. How the chair of the Federal Reserve's Board of Governors is appointed: _____

   _____

   _____

4. The function of each Federal Reserve Bank: _____

   _____

5. The makeup of each Federal Reserve Bank's board of directors: _____

   _____

6. Which banks join the Federal Reserve System and why they join: _____

   _____

7. The main function of the Federal Reserve's Federal Advisory Council: _____

   _____

   _____

8. Areas affected by announcements from the Federal Open Market Committee: _____

   _____

   _____

B. Reviewing Key Terms

Define the following terms.

9. monetary policy _____

   _____

10. Federal Reserve Districts _____

   _____

11. Federal Advisory Council _____

   _____

12. Federal Open Market Committee _____

   _____

Section 2: Guided Reading and Review
Federal Reserve Functions

A. As You Read

As you read Section 2, complete each numbered item in the chart.

The Federal Reserve in Action	
Service Roles	**Regulatory Roles**
1. sells, transfers, and redeems	8. collects daily reports on banks'
2. issues paper	9. may force banks to sell
3. acts as a clearing center for	10. may force problem banks to undergo
4. checks up on activities of member banks by sending out	11. subjects banks that go to the Fed for emergency loans too often to
5. uses findings and recommendations of Reserve Banks to approve or disapprove	12. regulates the nation's
6. protects consumers by enforcing	13. compares M1, M2, and M3 measurements with the likely
7. in severe recessions, provides commercial banks with	14. uses its tools to try to stabilize the nation's overall

B. Reviewing Key Terms

Complete each sentence by writing the correct term in the blank.

15. When a bank borrows money from another bank, the interest rate it pays is called the _____.

16. Ownership of more than one bank constitutes a _____.

17. When a bank customer writes a check, the check will go through the process of _____.

18. A bank's total assets minus its total liabilities make up its _____.

19. Banks repay loans from the Federal Reserve at a rate of interest called the _____.

Section 3: Guided Reading and Review
Monetary Policy Tools

A. As You Read

As you read Section 3, answer the following questions.

1. If you deposit $1,000 of borrowed money in a bank checking account, by how much do you increase the money supply? _____

2. Why does the Federal Reserve establish a required reserve ratio? _____
_____

3. What three tools could the Federal Reserve use to adjust the money supply? _____
_____

4. What two effects, leading to an increased money supply, could a reduced RRR have?
_____

5. Why does the Fed seldom, if ever, change bank reserve requirements? _____
_____

6. How do banks respond to a lowered discount rate? _____
_____

7. How does a raised discount rate affect bank loans and the money supply? _____
_____

8. What effect does the Fed's purchase of government bonds have on the money supply?
_____

9. How does the Fed's sale of bonds reduce the money supply? _____
_____
_____

10. Which of its monetary policy tools does the Federal Reserve use most often? _____
_____

B. Reviewing Key Terms

Rewrite each statement below as needed to make it correct.

11. *Money creation* is the process by which money is manufactured. _____
_____

12. The *required reserve ratio* is the ratio of reserves to loans required of banks by the Federal
Reserve. _____
_____

13. The size of loans created with each demand deposit is measured by the *money multiplier
formula.* _____
_____

14. *Open market operations* refers to the buying and selling of banks by the Federal Reserve.
_____
_____

Section 4: Guided Reading and Review

Monetary Policy and Macroeconomic Stabilization

A. As You Read

As you read Section 4, complete the following sentences.

1. The cost of borrowing or having money is the _____.

2. If the money supply is high, interest rates will be _____.

3. Lower interest rates give firms more opportunities for _____.

4. The Fed may follow an easy money policy when the macroeconomy is experiencing a _____.

5. The Fed may follow a tight money policy when the macroeconomy is experiencing a _____.

6. The goal of stabilization policy is to smooth out fluctuations in the _____.

7. If expansionary policies take effect while the macroeconomy is already expanding, the result could be higher _____.

8. One reason for inside lags is that it takes time to _____.

9. A second reason for inside lags is that it can take additional time to _____.

10. Monetary policy can be put in place almost immediately by the _____.

11. The outside lag can be relatively short for _____ policy.

12. Outside lags for monetary policy can be lengthy because they primarily affect _____.

13. We rely more on the Fed to combat the business cycle because fiscal policy is often delayed by _____.

14. Economists who usually recommend enacting fiscal and monetary policies believe that economies _____.

B. Reviewing Key Terms

Define the following terms.

15. monetarism _____

_____

16. easy money policy _____

_____

17. tight money policy _____

_____

18. inside lag _____

_____

19. outside lag _____

_____

Section 1: Guided Reading and Review
Why Nations Trade

A. As You Read

As you read Section 1, answer the following questions about international trade in the spaces provided.

1. What resources are major influences on a country's or region's economy? _____
   _____
   _____

2. Why do countries differ in their capacities to produce different goods and services?
   _____
   _____

3. Why do specializing nations need world trade? _____
   _____
   _____

4. Why does trade benefit both countries with abundance and countries with few resources?
   _____
   _____

5. How do nations benefit from producing goods and services they have a comparative
   advantage in supplying? _____
   _____
   _____

6. How can international specialization affect some workers? _____
   _____
   _____

7. What possibilities do laid-off workers face? _____
   _____
   _____

B. Reviewing Key Terms

Briefly define or identify each of the following.

8. absolute advantage _____

9. export _____

10. import _____

11. comparative advantage _____

Section 2: Guided Reading and Review
Trade Barriers and Agreements

A. As You Read
As you read Section 2, supply the missing information in the spaces provided.

Current World Trade Considerations

1. Effects of Trade Barriers: _____

_____

_____

2. Presumed Advantages of U.S. Protectionism: _____

_____

_____

3. Progress Under GATT and WTO: _____

_____

_____

4. Results of NAFTA in the United States: _____

_____

_____

5. Advantages of Multinational Corporations: _____

_____

_____

B. Reviewing Key Terms
Match the definitions in Column I with the terms in Column II. Write the letter of the correct answer in the blank provided. You will not use all of the terms.

Column I

_____ 6. use of trade barriers to shield a nation's industries from foreign competition

_____ 7. regional trade organization of 15 European nations

_____ 8. self-imposed limitation on the number of products shipped to a particular country

_____ 9. means of preventing a foreign product or service from freely entering a nation's territory

_____ 10. limit on the amount of a good that can be brought into a country

_____ 11. region where a group of countries agrees to reduce or eliminate trade barriers

_____ 12. tax on imports

Column II

a. European Union (EU)

b. infant industry

c. trade barrier

d. NAFTA

e. tariff

f. World Trade Organization (WTO)

g. import quota

h. voluntary export restraint

i. free-trade zone

j. protectionism

Section 3: Guided Reading and Review
Measuring Trade

A. As You Read

As you read Section 3, supply likely consequences or solutions in the chart.

In Matters of International Trade

If	Then
1. a U.S. tourist wants to buy a newspaper in Beijing	1.
2. you want to learn current exchange rates	2.
3. a strong dollar makes American products more expensive in Japan	3.
4. the dollar is devalued	4.
5. an American firm needs to exchange yen for dollars	5.
6. low labor costs abroad result in lower prices for U.S. imports	6.

B. Reviewing Key Terms

Briefly explain the difference between the terms in each pair.

7. fixed exchange-rate system and flexible exchange-rate system _____

_____

8. trade surplus and trade deficit _____

_____

9. appreciation and depreciation _____

_____

Section 1: Guided Reading and Review
Levels of Development

A. As You Read

As you read Section 1, fill in details comparing characteristics of developed nations and less developed countries in the blanks provided.

	Developed Nations	**Less Developed Countries**
per capita GDP	1. _____	2. _____
energy consumption	3. _____	4. _____
labor force	5. _____	6. _____
literacy	7. _____	8. _____
life expectancy & infant mortality	9. _____	10. _____

B. Reviewing Key Terms

Match the descriptions in Column I with the terms in Column II. Write the letter of the correct answer in the blank provided.

Column I

_____ 11. services and facilities necessary for an economy to function

_____ 12. country with low levels of material well-being

_____ 13. a nation's GDP divided by its total population

_____ 14. more successful less developed country

_____ 15. raising just enough food to feed one's family

_____ 16. average expected life span of an individual

_____ 17. process by which a nation improves the economic, political, and social well-being of its people

_____ 18. proportion of the population over age 15 that can read and write

_____ 19. country with a higher average level of material well-being

_____ 20. the number of deaths that occur in the first year of life per 1,000 live births

_____ 21. extensive organization of an economy for the purpose of manufacture

Column II

a. development

b. subsistence agriculture

c. infant mortality rate

d. industrialization

e. developed nation

f. infrastructure

g. life expectancy

h. newly industrialized country (NIC)

i. literacy rate

j. per capita gross domestic product (per capita GDP)

k. less developed country

NAME _____ CLASS _____ DATE _____

A. As You Read

As you read Section 2, supply the missing effects of problems suffered by less developed countries in the spaces provided.

Cause: Rapid population growth
1. Effect: _____

Cause: Uneven global distribution of resources
2. Effect: _____

Cause: Lack of physical capital
3. Effect: _____

Cause: Lack of human capital
4. Effect: _____
5. Effect: _____

Cause: Colonial dependency
6. Effect: _____

Cause: Government corruption
7. Effect: _____

Cause: Political instability
8. Effect: _____

Cause: 1973 OPEC price increase
9. Effect: _____

B. Reviewing Key Terms

Complete each sentence by writing the correct term in the blank.

10. Land suitable for producing crops is considered _____.

11. The increase in a country's population in a given year is called the _____.

12. The difference between a country's death rate and birth rate is called the

_____.

13. People who get too little nutritional food suffer from _____.

Section 3: Guided Reading and Review
Financing Development

A. As You Read

As you read Section 3, supply the missing information in the spaces provided.

List three advantages economists believe multinational corporations bring to LDCs.

1. _____

2. _____

3. _____

List three disadvantages economists believe multinational corporations bring to LDCs.

4. _____

5. _____

6. _____

Give an example of why nations provide aid to less developed countries.

Humanitarian:

7. _____

Political and Military:

8. _____

9. _____

B. Reviewing Key Terms

Define the following terms.

10. internal financing _____

11. foreign investment _____

12. foreign direct investment (FDI) _____

13. foreign portfolio investment _____

14. United Nations Development Program (UNDP) _____

_____

15. World Bank _____

16. International Monetary Fund (IMF) _____

_____

17. debt rescheduling _____

_____

18. stabilization program _____

_____

Section 4: Guided Reading and Review
Transitions to Free Enterprise

A. As You Read

As you read Section 4, provide details for each numbered item in the sequence chains below to show the series of events leading toward a free market economy in Russia.

Transition in Russia

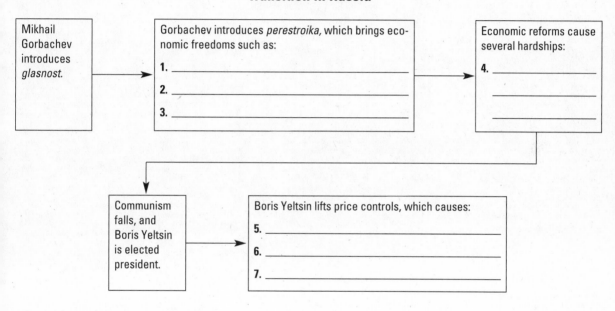

Mikhail Gorbachev introduces *glasnost*.	Gorbachev introduces *perestroika,* which brings economic freedoms such as: 1. _____ 2. _____ 3. _____

Economic reforms cause several hardships:
4. _____
_____
_____

Communism falls, and Boris Yeltsin is elected president.

Boris Yeltsin lifts price controls, which causes:
5. _____
6. _____
7. _____

B. Reviewing Key Terms

Answer each of the following questions.

8. Why is the work ethic important to a system of privatization? _____
_____
_____

9. How are *glasnost* and *perestroika* related to free enterprise? _____
_____
_____

10. How did the focus on light industry benefit consumers? _____
_____
_____

11. How did economic growth in China's special economic zones compare to economic growth in the interior regions? _____
_____